I0482344

MAINTENANCE LOG

Log Book Number ______________

Continued From Log Book Number ______________

Continued to Log Book Number ______________

Assigned To:

Name ______________________________

Signature ______________________________

Date ______________________________

Date Issued ______________________________

Issued By ______________________________

Phone ______________________________

Email ______________________________

Company ______________________________

Department ______________________________

Address ______________________________

Mail Stop ______________________________

City ______________________________

State ______________________________

ZIP ______________________________

Date Log Book Completed ______________________________

Number of Log Book Pages Completed ______________________________

Notes:

MAINTENANCE LOG BOOK

Log Book #______________

Date / Time	Maintenance / Comments	Signature

MAINTENANCE LOG BOOK

Log Book #______________

Date / Time	Maintenance / Comments	Signature

MAINTENANCE LOG BOOK

Log Book #______________

Date / Time	Maintenance / Comments	Signature

MAINTENANCE LOG BOOK

Log Book #______________

Date / Time	Maintenance / Comments	Signature

MAINTENANCE LOG BOOK

Log Book #______________

Date / Time	Maintenance / Comments	Signature

MAINTENANCE LOG BOOK

Log Book #______________

Date / Time	Maintenance / Comments	Signature

MAINTENANCE LOG BOOK

Log Book #______________

Date / Time	Maintenance / Comments	Signature

MAINTENANCE LOG BOOK

Log Book #______________

Date / Time	Maintenance / Comments	Signature

MAINTENANCE LOG BOOK

Log Book #______________

Date / Time	Maintenance / Comments	Signature

MAINTENANCE LOG BOOK

Log Book #_____________

Date / Time	Maintenance / Comments	Signature

MAINTENANCE LOG BOOK

Log Book #_____________

Date / Time	Maintenance / Comments	Signature

MAINTENANCE LOG BOOK

Log Book #______________

Date / Time	Maintenance / Comments	Signature

MAINTENANCE LOG BOOK

Log Book #____________

Date / Time	Maintenance / Comments	Signature

MAINTENANCE LOG BOOK

Log Book #______________

Date / Time	Maintenance / Comments	Signature

MAINTENANCE LOG BOOK

Log Book #______________

Date / Time	Maintenance / Comments	Signature

MAINTENANCE LOG BOOK

Log Book #____________

Date / Time	Maintenance / Comments	Signature

MAINTENANCE LOG BOOK

Log Book #______________

Date / Time	Maintenance / Comments	Signature

MAINTENANCE LOG BOOK

Log Book #____________

Date / Time	Maintenance / Comments	Signature

MAINTENANCE LOG BOOK

Log Book #_____________

Date / Time	Maintenance / Comments	Signature

MAINTENANCE LOG BOOK

Log Book #______________

Date / Time	Maintenance / Comments	Signature

MAINTENANCE LOG BOOK

Log Book #______________

Date / Time	Maintenance / Comments	Signature

MAINTENANCE LOG BOOK

Log Book #_____________

Date / Time	Maintenance / Comments	Signature

MAINTENANCE LOG BOOK

Log Book #______________

Date / Time	Maintenance / Comments	Signature

MAINTENANCE LOG BOOK

Log Book #______________

Date / Time	Maintenance / Comments	Signature

MAINTENANCE LOG BOOK

Log Book #______________

Date / Time	Maintenance / Comments	Signature

MAINTENANCE LOG BOOK

Log Book #____________

Date / Time	Maintenance / Comments	Signature

MAINTENANCE LOG BOOK

Log Book #______________

Date / Time	Maintenance / Comments	Signature

MAINTENANCE LOG BOOK

Log Book #______________

Date / Time	Maintenance / Comments	Signature

MAINTENANCE LOG BOOK

Log Book #______________

Date / Time	Maintenance / Comments	Signature

MAINTENANCE LOG BOOK

Log Book #_____________

Date / Time	Maintenance / Comments	Signature

MAINTENANCE LOG BOOK

Log Book #______________

Date / Time	Maintenance / Comments	Signature

MAINTENANCE LOG BOOK

Log Book #______________

Date / Time	Maintenance / Comments	Signature

MAINTENANCE LOG BOOK

Log Book #______________

Date / Time	Maintenance / Comments	Signature

MAINTENANCE LOG BOOK

Log Book #______________

Date / Time	Maintenance / Comments	Signature

MAINTENANCE LOG BOOK

Log Book #______________

Date / Time	Maintenance / Comments	Signature

MAINTENANCE LOG BOOK

Log Book #______________

Date / Time	Maintenance / Comments	Signature

MAINTENANCE LOG BOOK

Log Book #______________

Date / Time	Maintenance / Comments	Signature

MAINTENANCE LOG BOOK

Log Book #_____________

Date / Time	Maintenance / Comments	Signature

MAINTENANCE LOG BOOK

Log Book #______________

Date / Time	Maintenance / Comments	Signature

MAINTENANCE LOG BOOK

Log Book #_____________

Date / Time	Maintenance / Comments	Signature

MAINTENANCE LOG BOOK

Log Book #______________

Date / Time	Maintenance / Comments	Signature

MAINTENANCE LOG BOOK

Log Book #_____________

Date / Time	Maintenance / Comments	Signature

MAINTENANCE LOG BOOK

Log Book #______________

Date / Time	Maintenance / Comments	Signature

MAINTENANCE LOG BOOK

Log Book #_____________

Date / Time	Maintenance / Comments	Signature

MAINTENANCE LOG BOOK

Log Book #_____________

Date / Time	Maintenance / Comments	Signature

MAINTENANCE LOG BOOK

Log Book #______________

Date / Time	Maintenance / Comments	Signature

MAINTENANCE LOG BOOK

Log Book #______________

Date / Time	Maintenance / Comments	Signature

MAINTENANCE LOG BOOK

Log Book #______________

Date / Time	Maintenance / Comments	Signature

MAINTENANCE LOG BOOK

Log Book #______________

Date / Time	Maintenance / Comments	Signature

MAINTENANCE LOG BOOK

Log Book #_____________

Date / Time	Maintenance / Comments	Signature

MAINTENANCE LOG BOOK

Log Book #______________

Date / Time	Maintenance / Comments	Signature

MAINTENANCE LOG BOOK

Log Book #____________

Date / Time	Maintenance / Comments	Signature

MAINTENANCE LOG BOOK

Log Book #______________

Date / Time	Maintenance / Comments	Signature

MAINTENANCE LOG BOOK

Log Book #____________

Date / Time	Maintenance / Comments	Signature

MAINTENANCE LOG BOOK

Log Book #______________

Date / Time	Maintenance / Comments	Signature

MAINTENANCE LOG BOOK

Log Book #______________

Date / Time	Maintenance / Comments	Signature

MAINTENANCE LOG BOOK

Log Book #______________

Date / Time	Maintenance / Comments	Signature

MAINTENANCE LOG BOOK

Log Book #______________

Date / Time	Maintenance / Comments	Signature

MAINTENANCE LOG BOOK

Log Book #______________

Date / Time	Maintenance / Comments	Signature

MAINTENANCE LOG BOOK

Log Book #______________

Date / Time	Maintenance / Comments	Signature

MAINTENANCE LOG BOOK

Log Book #_____________

Date / Time	Maintenance / Comments	Signature

MAINTENANCE LOG BOOK

Log Book #______________

Date / Time	Maintenance / Comments	Signature

MAINTENANCE LOG BOOK

Log Book #______________

Date / Time	Maintenance / Comments	Signature

MAINTENANCE LOG BOOK

Log Book #______________

Date / Time	Maintenance / Comments	Signature

MAINTENANCE LOG BOOK

Log Book #______________

Date / Time	Maintenance / Comments	Signature

MAINTENANCE LOG BOOK

Log Book #______________

Date / Time	Maintenance / Comments	Signature

MAINTENANCE LOG BOOK

Log Book #______________

Date / Time	Maintenance / Comments	Signature

MAINTENANCE LOG BOOK

Log Book #_____________

Date / Time	Maintenance / Comments	Signature

MAINTENANCE LOG BOOK

Log Book #______________

Date / Time	Maintenance / Comments	Signature

MAINTENANCE LOG BOOK

Log Book #____________

Date / Time	Maintenance / Comments	Signature

MAINTENANCE LOG BOOK

Log Book #______________

Date / Time	Maintenance / Comments	Signature

MAINTENANCE LOG BOOK

Log Book #_____________

Date / Time	Maintenance / Comments	Signature

MAINTENANCE LOG BOOK

Log Book #______________

Date / Time	Maintenance / Comments	Signature

MAINTENANCE LOG BOOK

Log Book #_____________

Date / Time	Maintenance / Comments	Signature

MAINTENANCE LOG BOOK

Log Book #______________

Date / Time	Maintenance / Comments	Signature

MAINTENANCE LOG BOOK

Log Book #______________

Date / Time	Maintenance / Comments	Signature

MAINTENANCE LOG BOOK

Log Book #______________

Date / Time	Maintenance / Comments	Signature

MAINTENANCE LOG BOOK

Log Book #____________

Date / Time	Maintenance / Comments	Signature

MAINTENANCE LOG BOOK

Log Book #______________

Date / Time	Maintenance / Comments	Signature

MAINTENANCE LOG BOOK

Log Book #_____________

Date / Time	Maintenance / Comments	Signature

MAINTENANCE LOG BOOK

Log Book #______________

Date / Time	Maintenance / Comments	Signature

MAINTENANCE LOG BOOK

Log Book #______________

Date / Time	Maintenance / Comments	Signature

MAINTENANCE LOG BOOK

Log Book #______________

Date / Time	Maintenance / Comments	Signature

MAINTENANCE LOG BOOK

Log Book #______________

Date / Time	Maintenance / Comments	Signature

MAINTENANCE LOG BOOK

Log Book #______________

Date / Time	Maintenance / Comments	Signature

MAINTENANCE LOG BOOK

Log Book #_____________

Date / Time	Maintenance / Comments	Signature

MAINTENANCE LOG BOOK

Log Book #_____________

Date / Time	Maintenance / Comments	Signature

MAINTENANCE LOG BOOK

Log Book #______________

Date / Time	Maintenance / Comments	Signature

MAINTENANCE LOG BOOK

Log Book #______________

Date / Time	Maintenance / Comments	Signature

MAINTENANCE LOG BOOK

Log Book #______________

Date / Time	Maintenance / Comments	Signature

MAINTENANCE LOG BOOK

Log Book #______________

Date / Time	Maintenance / Comments	Signature

MAINTENANCE LOG BOOK

Log Book #_______________

Date / Time	Maintenance / Comments	Signature

MAINTENANCE LOG BOOK

Log Book #_____________

Date / Time	Maintenance / Comments	Signature

MAINTENANCE LOG BOOK

Log Book #______________

Date / Time	Maintenance / Comments	Signature

MAINTENANCE LOG BOOK

Log Book #______________

Date / Time	Maintenance / Comments	Signature

MAINTENANCE LOG BOOK

Log Book #_____________

Date / Time	Maintenance / Comments	Signature

MAINTENANCE LOG BOOK

Log Book #______________

Date / Time	Maintenance / Comments	Signature

MAINTENANCE LOG BOOK

Log Book #____________

Date / Time	Maintenance / Comments	Signature

MAINTENANCE LOG BOOK

Log Book #______________

Date / Time	Maintenance / Comments	Signature

MAINTENANCE LOG BOOK

Log Book #______________

Date / Time	Maintenance / Comments	Signature

MAINTENANCE LOG BOOK

Log Book #______________

Date / Time	Maintenance / Comments	Signature

MAINTENANCE LOG BOOK

Log Book #______________

Date / Time	Maintenance / Comments	Signature

MAINTENANCE LOG BOOK

Log Book #______________

Date / Time	Maintenance / Comments	Signature

MAINTENANCE LOG BOOK

Log Book #______________

Date / Time	Maintenance / Comments	Signature

MAINTENANCE LOG BOOK

Log Book #______________

Date / Time	Maintenance / Comments	Signature

MAINTENANCE LOG BOOK

Log Book #______________

Date / Time	Maintenance / Comments	Signature

MAINTENANCE LOG BOOK

Log Book #______________

Date / Time	Maintenance / Comments	Signature

MAINTENANCE LOG BOOK

Log Book #______________

Date / Time	Maintenance / Comments	Signature

MAINTENANCE LOG BOOK

Log Book #____________

Date / Time	Maintenance / Comments	Signature

MAINTENANCE LOG BOOK

Log Book #______________

Date / Time	Maintenance / Comments	Signature

www.ingramcontent.com/pod-product-compliance
Lightning Source LLC
Chambersburg PA
CBHW080706190526
45169CB00006B/2256
9781535078702